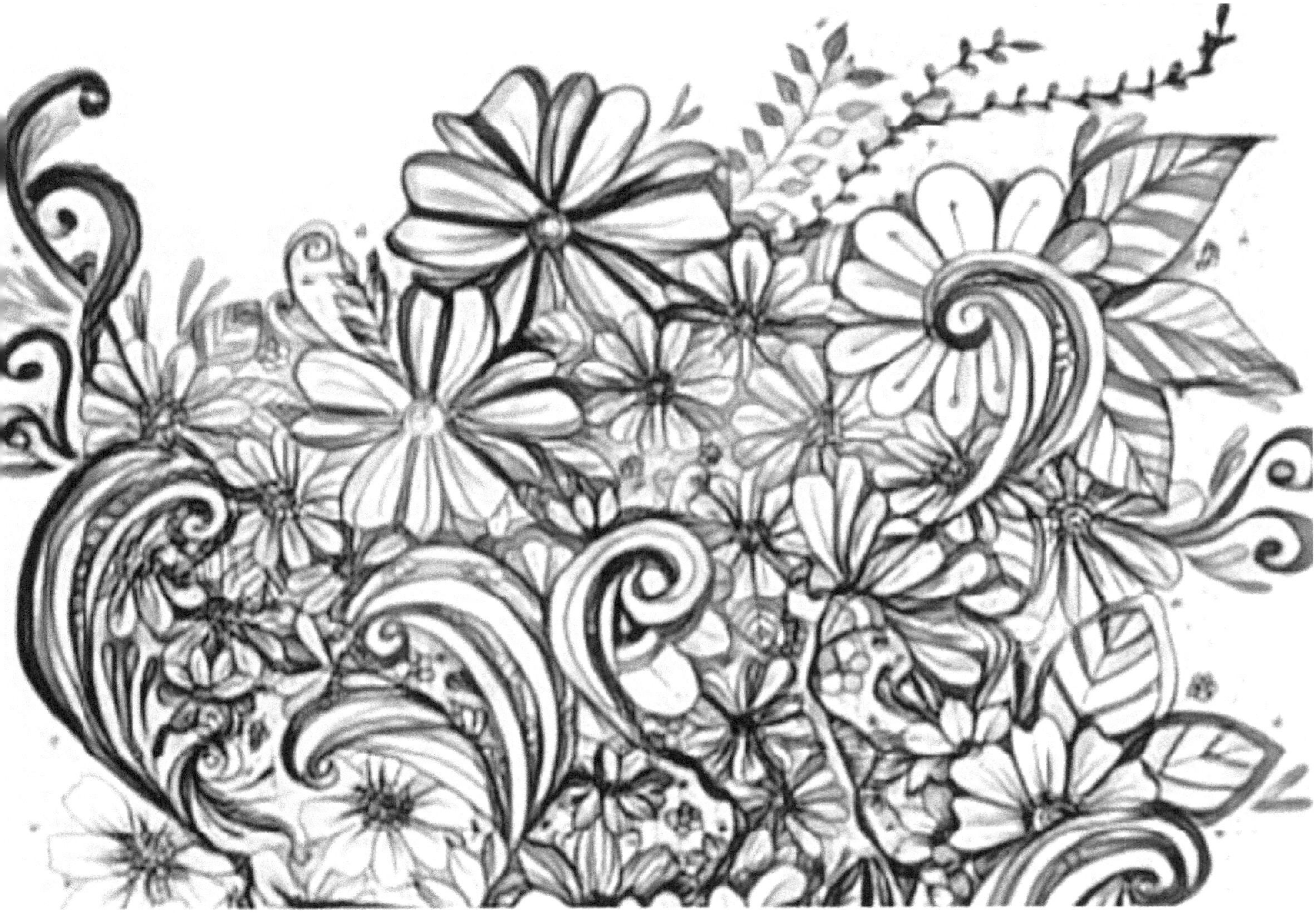

Mystical Nature

Calming Patterns Coloring Book.
Illustrated by: Thitima Alabi

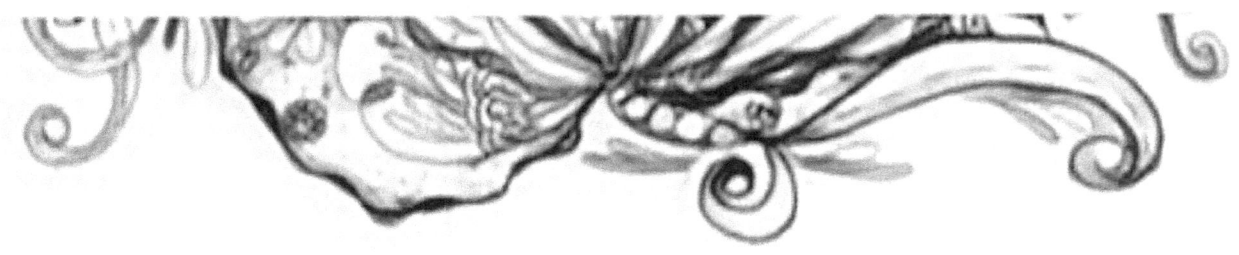

This book belongs to...

_____

_

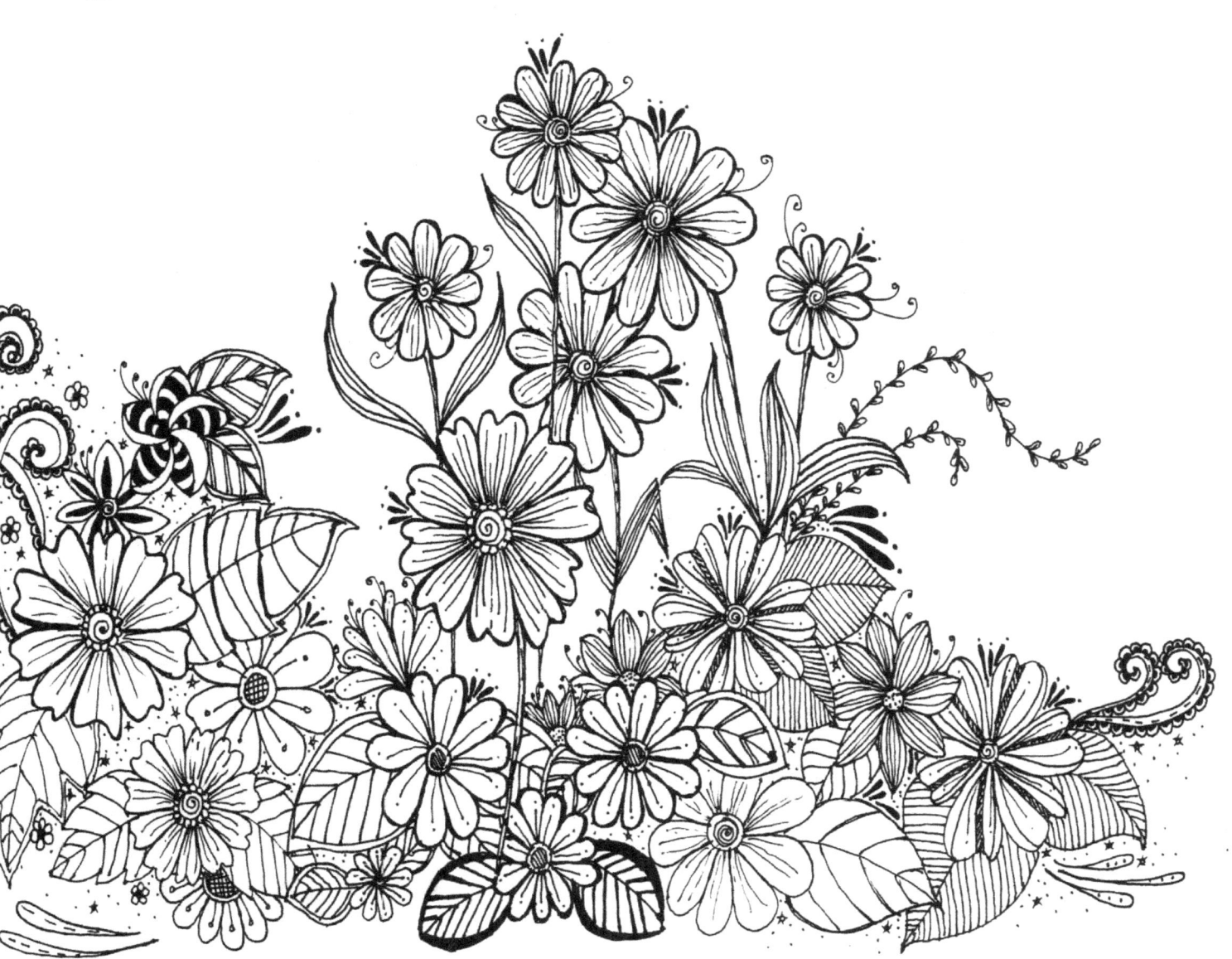

"Faith is the bird that feels the light
when the dawn is still dark."
~ Rabindranath Tagore

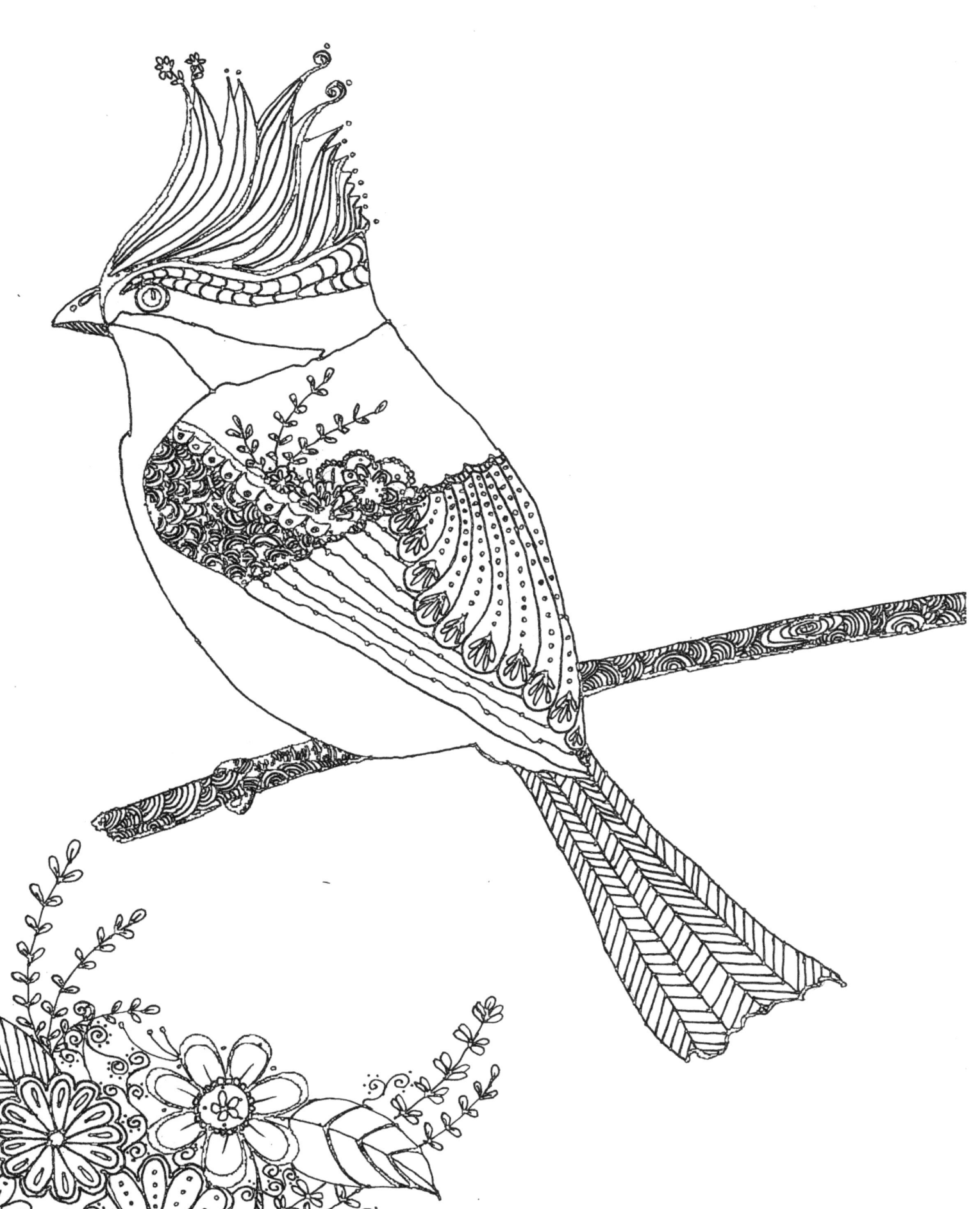

"All good things are wild and free."
~ *Henry David Thoreau*

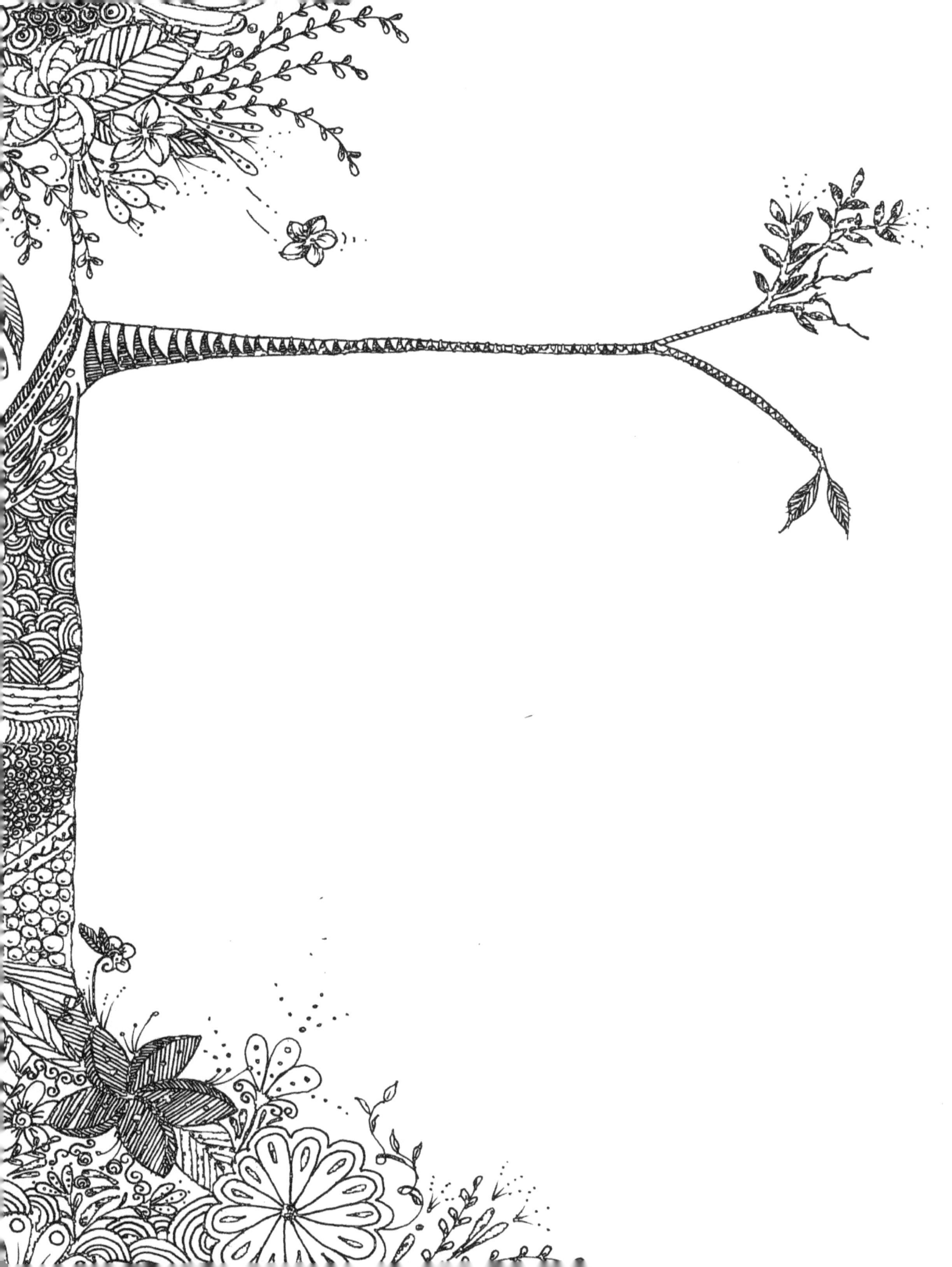

"The poetry of earth is never dead."
~ John Keats

" In every walk with nature
one receives far more than he seeks."
~ John Muir

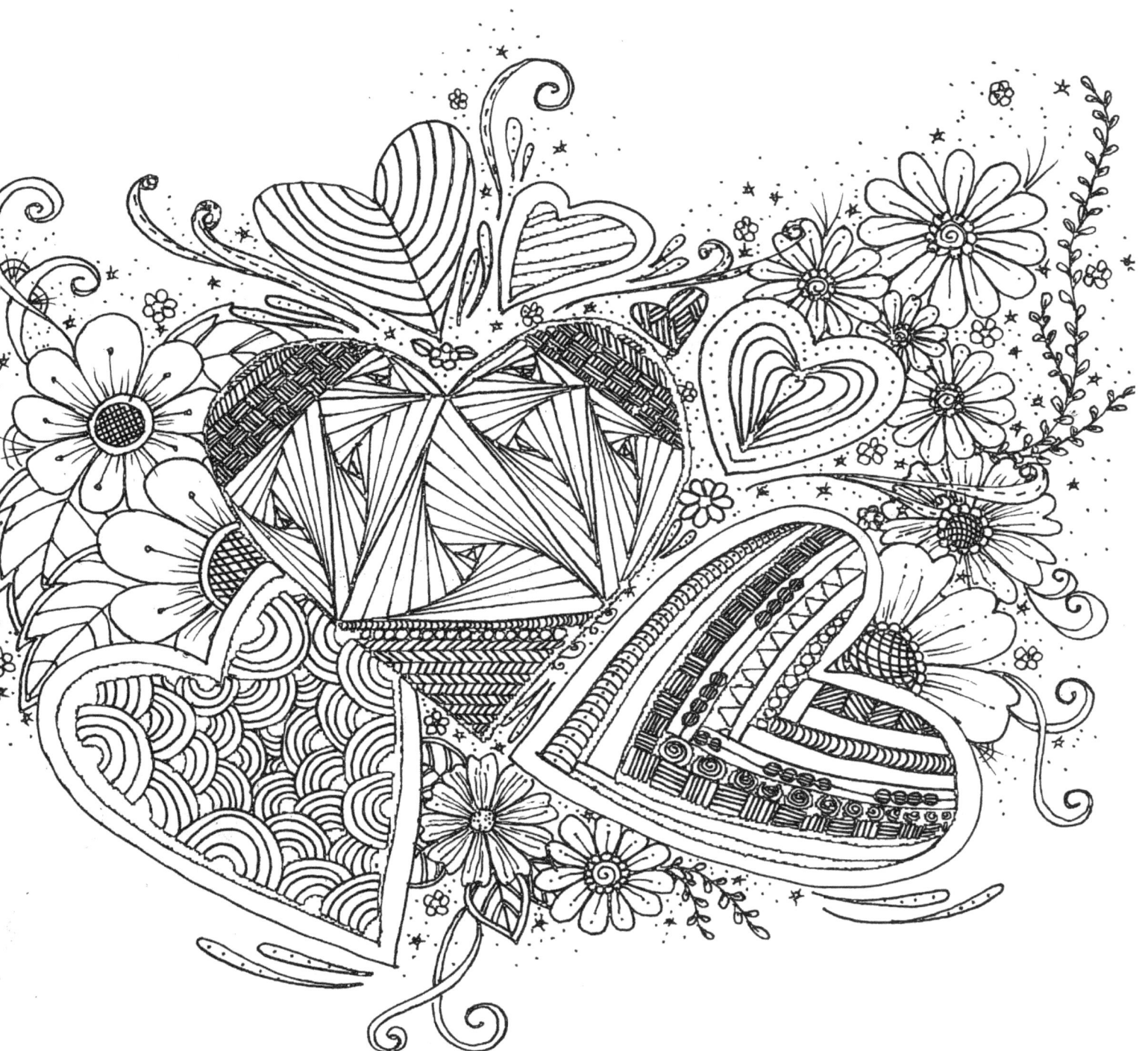

"Nature is not a place to visit. It is home."

~ Gary Snyder

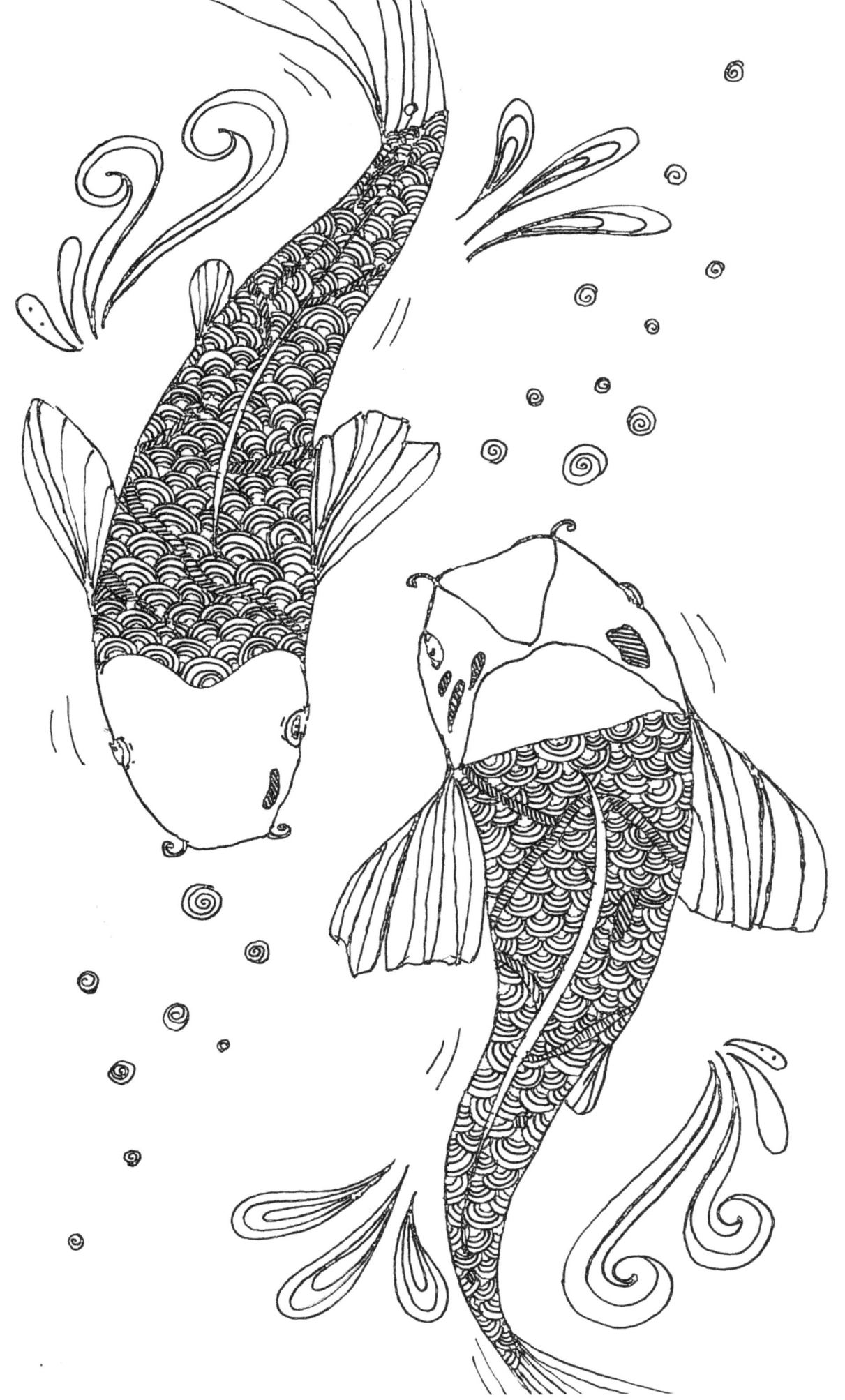

"If you truly love nature,
you will find beauty everywhere"
~ Vincent Van Gogh

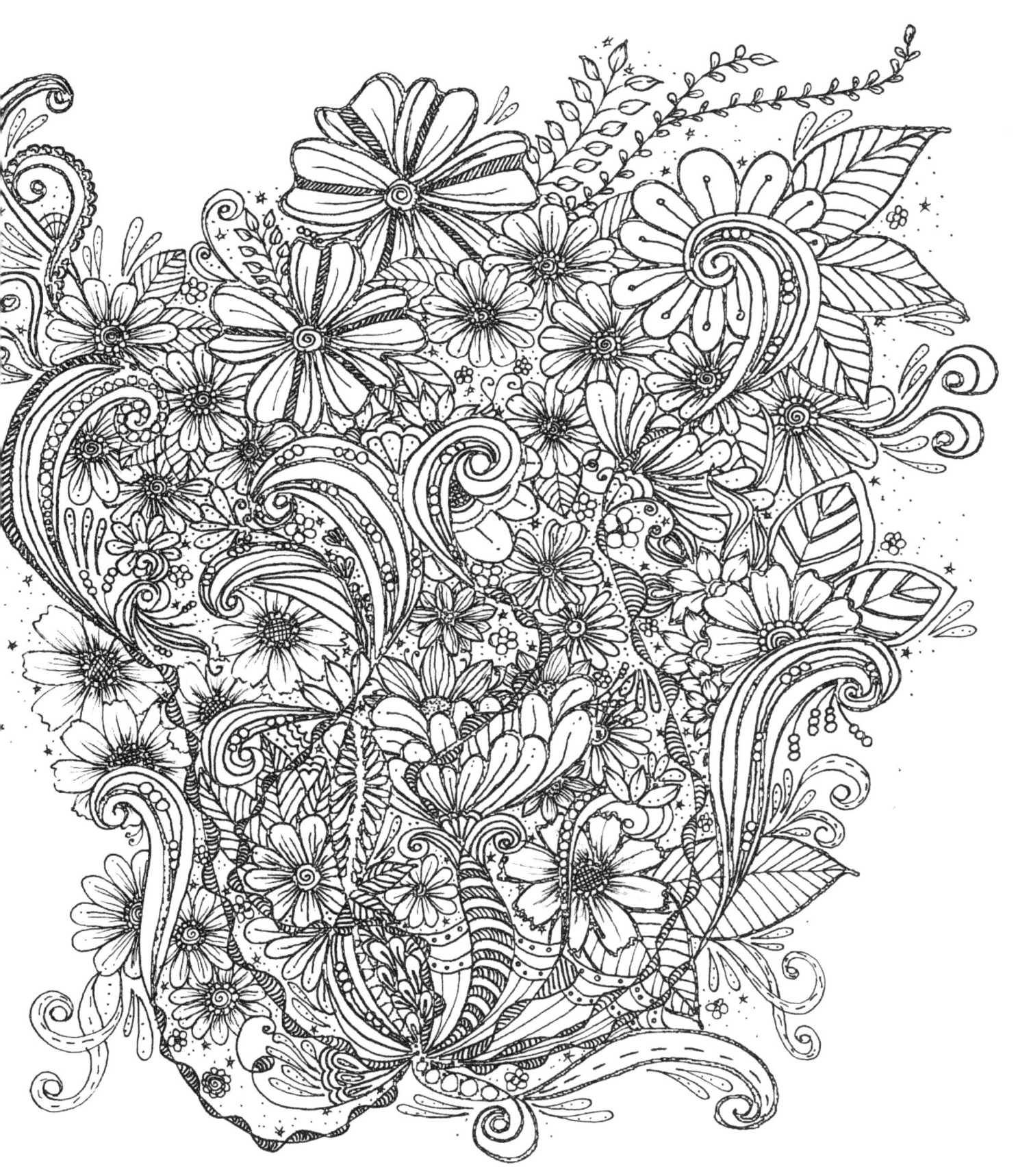

"All the trees are losing their leaves,
and not one of them is worried."
~ Donald Miller

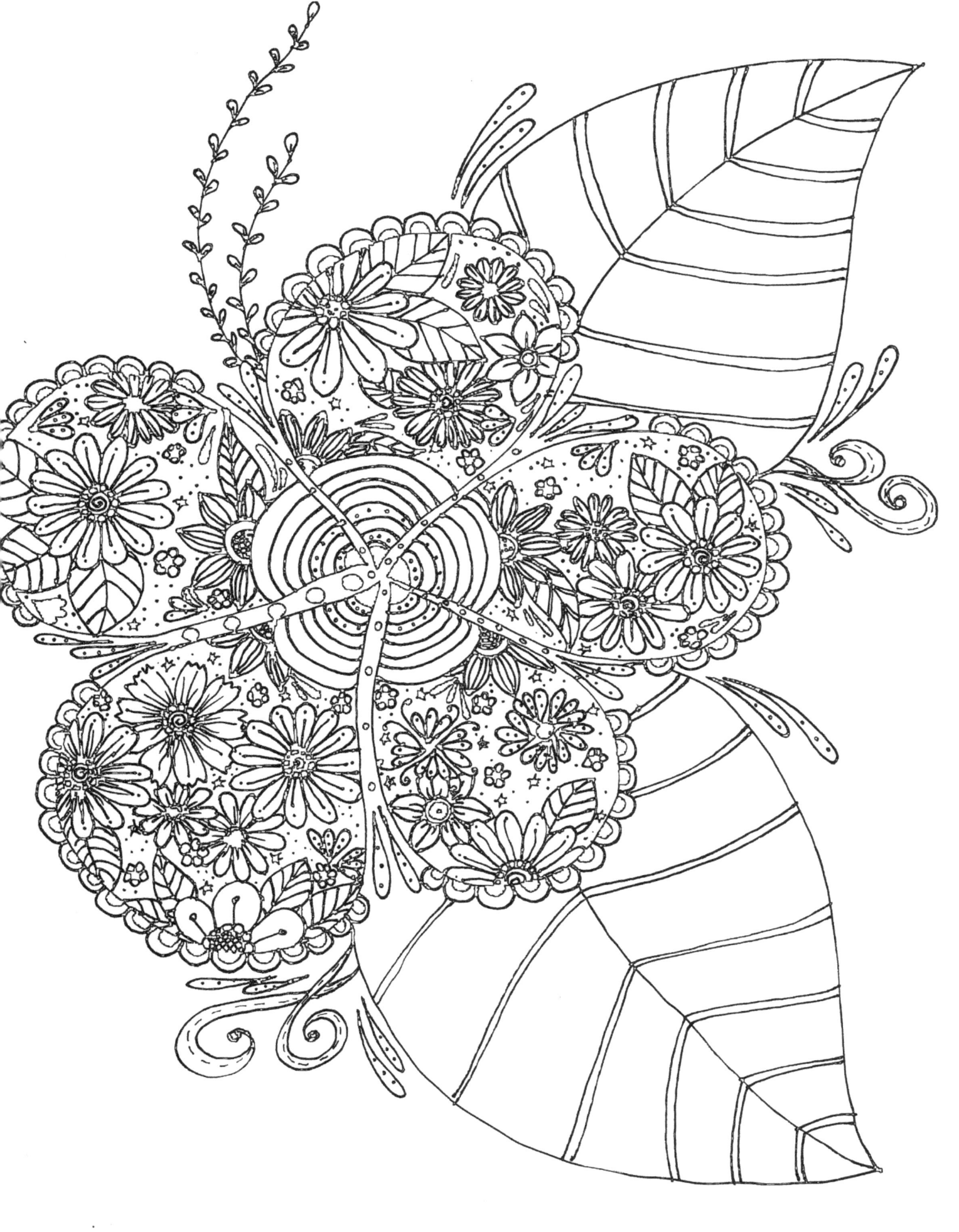

"All I have seen teaches me
to trust the Creator for all I have not seen."
~ Ralph Waldo Emerson

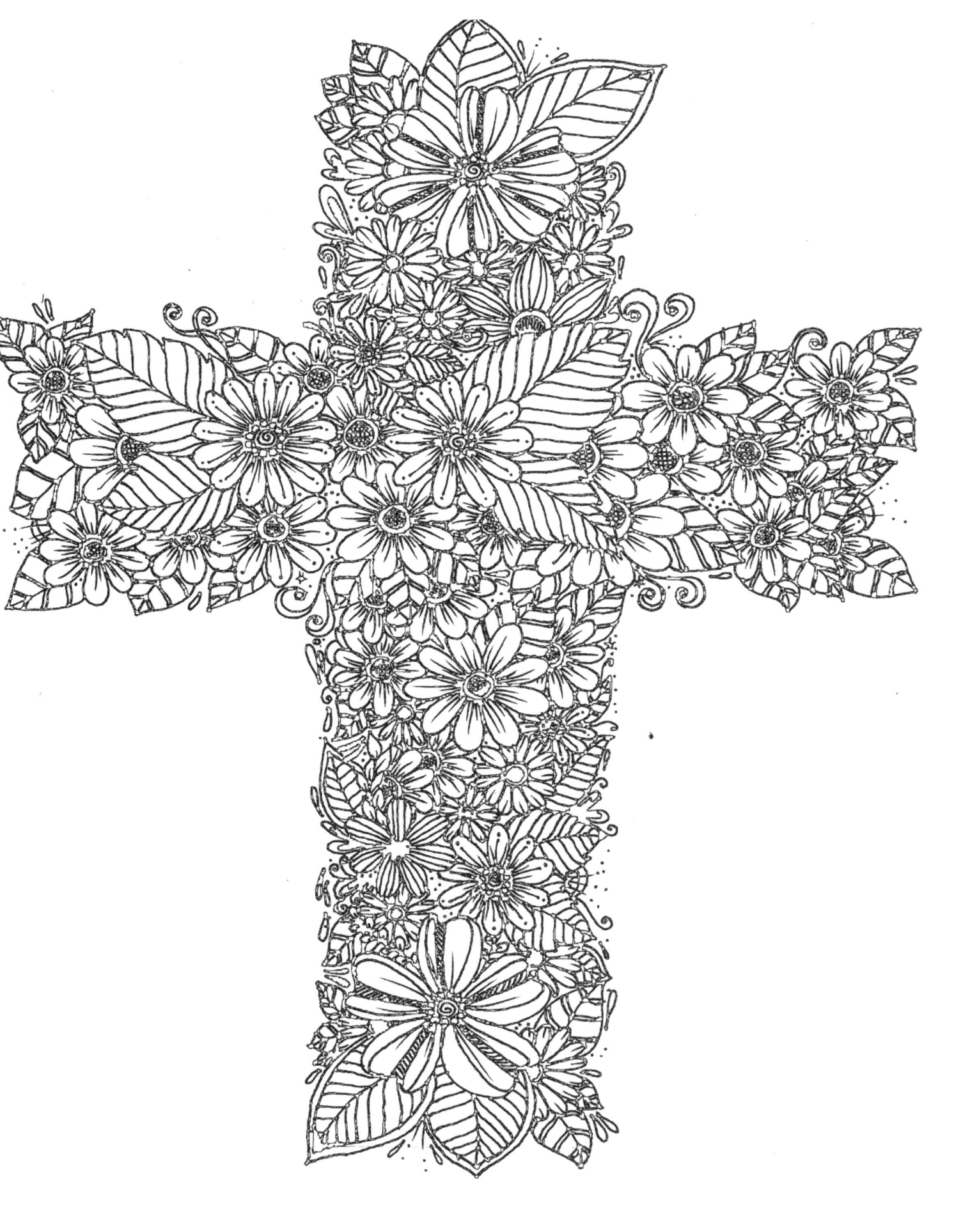

"Nature does not hurry, yet everything is accomplished."
~ Lao Tzu

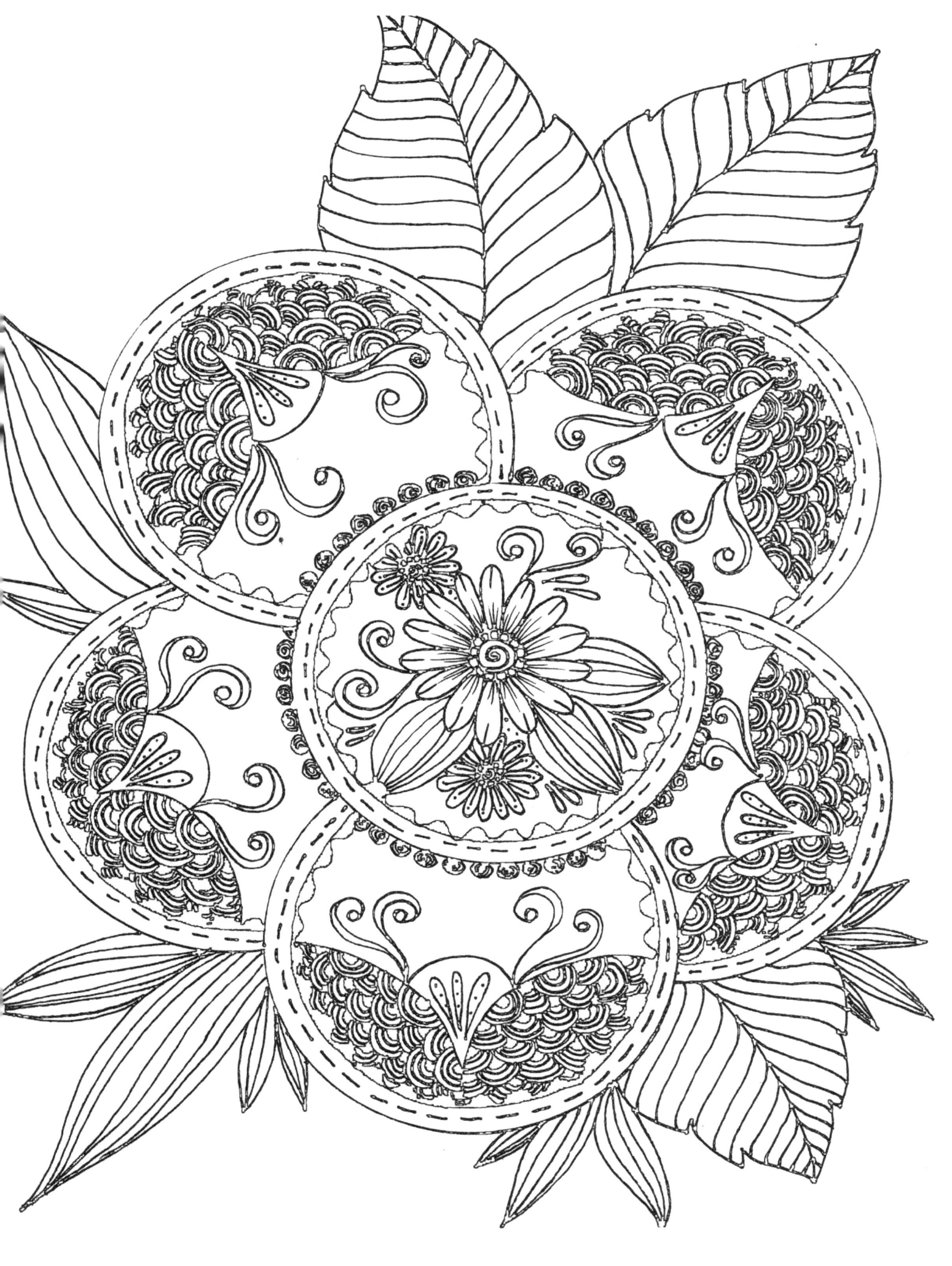

"*Adopt the pace of nature. Her secret is patience.*"
~ *Ralph Waldo Emerson*

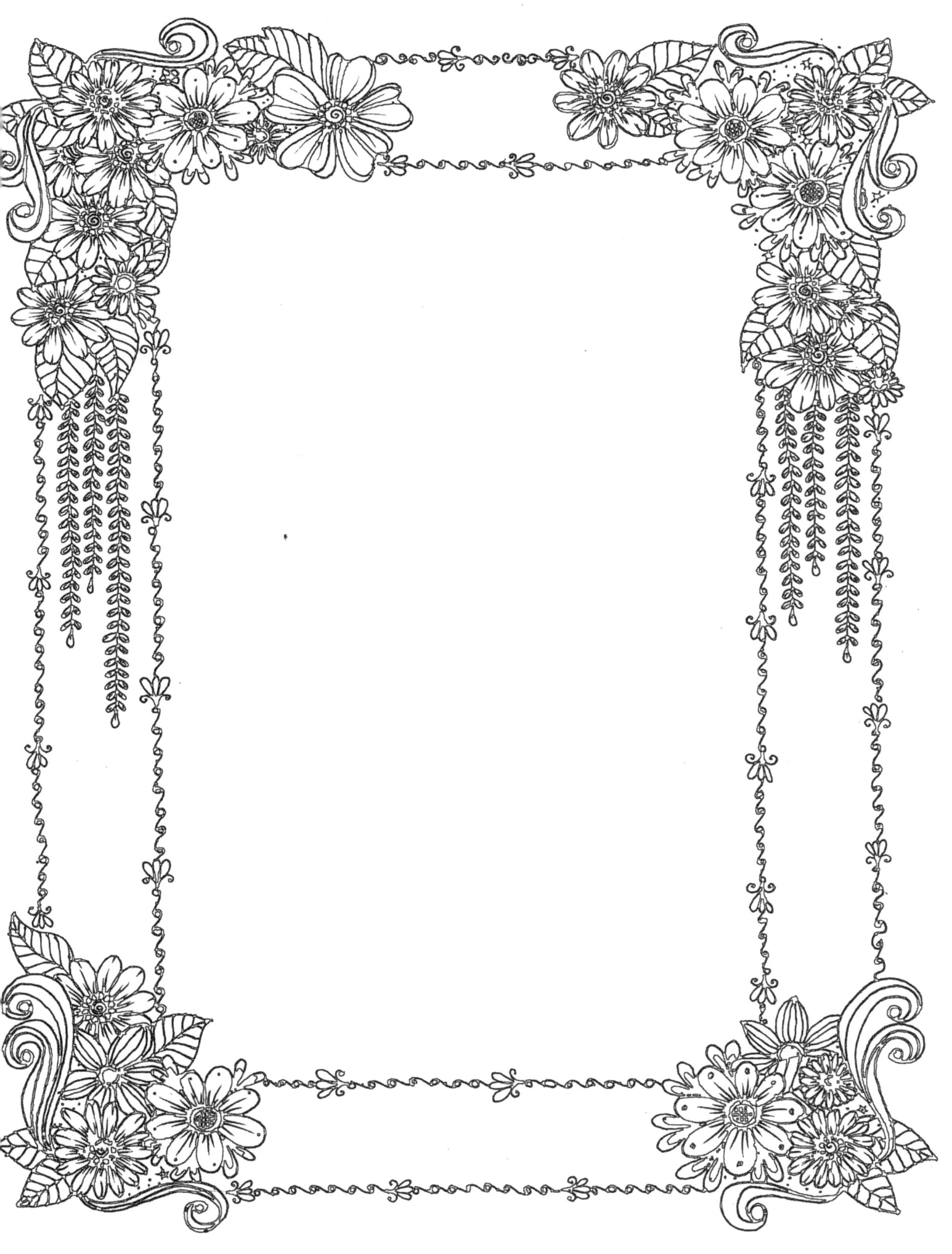

"May my soul bloom in love for all existence."
~ Rudolf Steiner

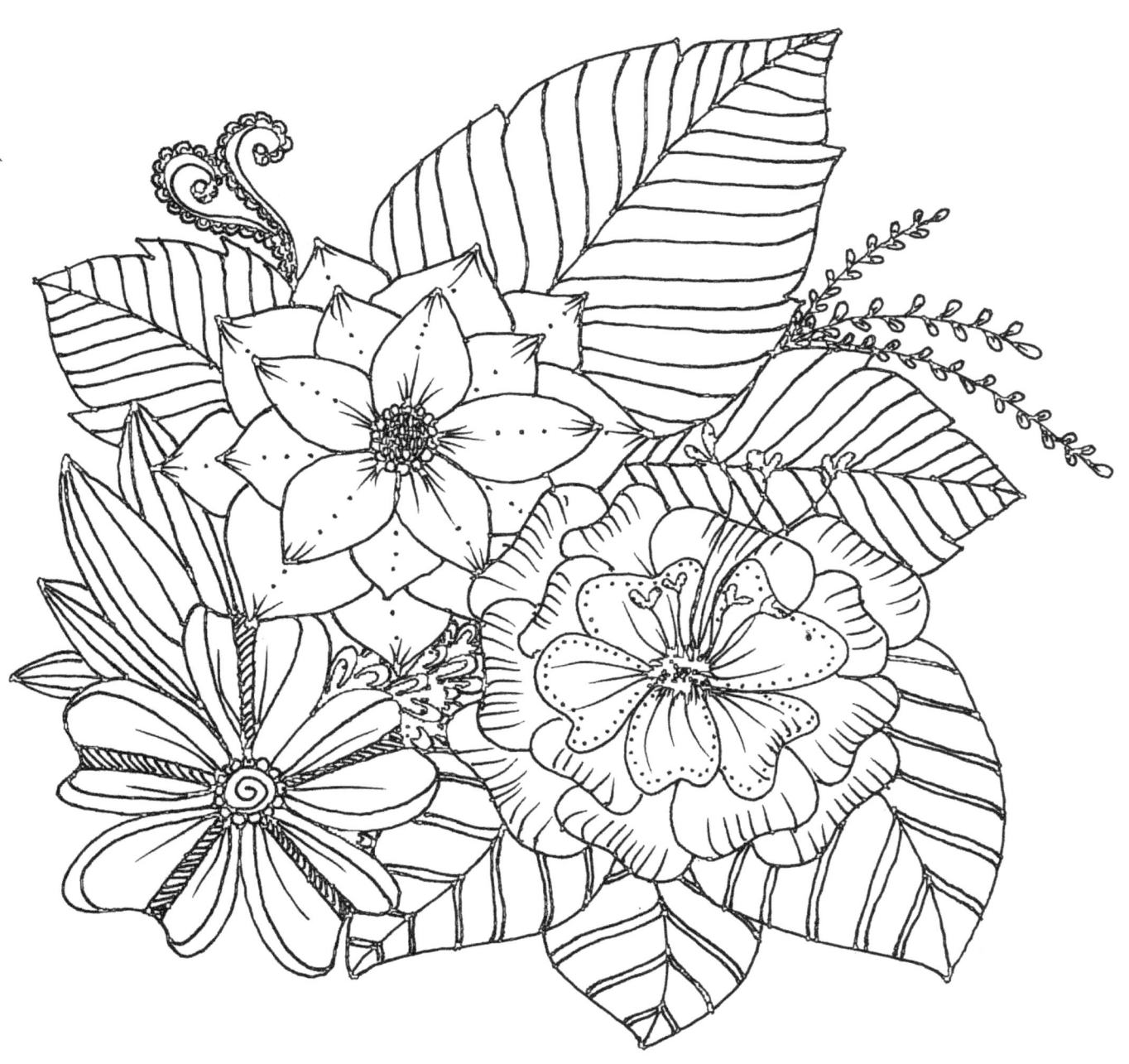

"With the wind of love, let your heart dance like a flower."
~ Debasish Mridha

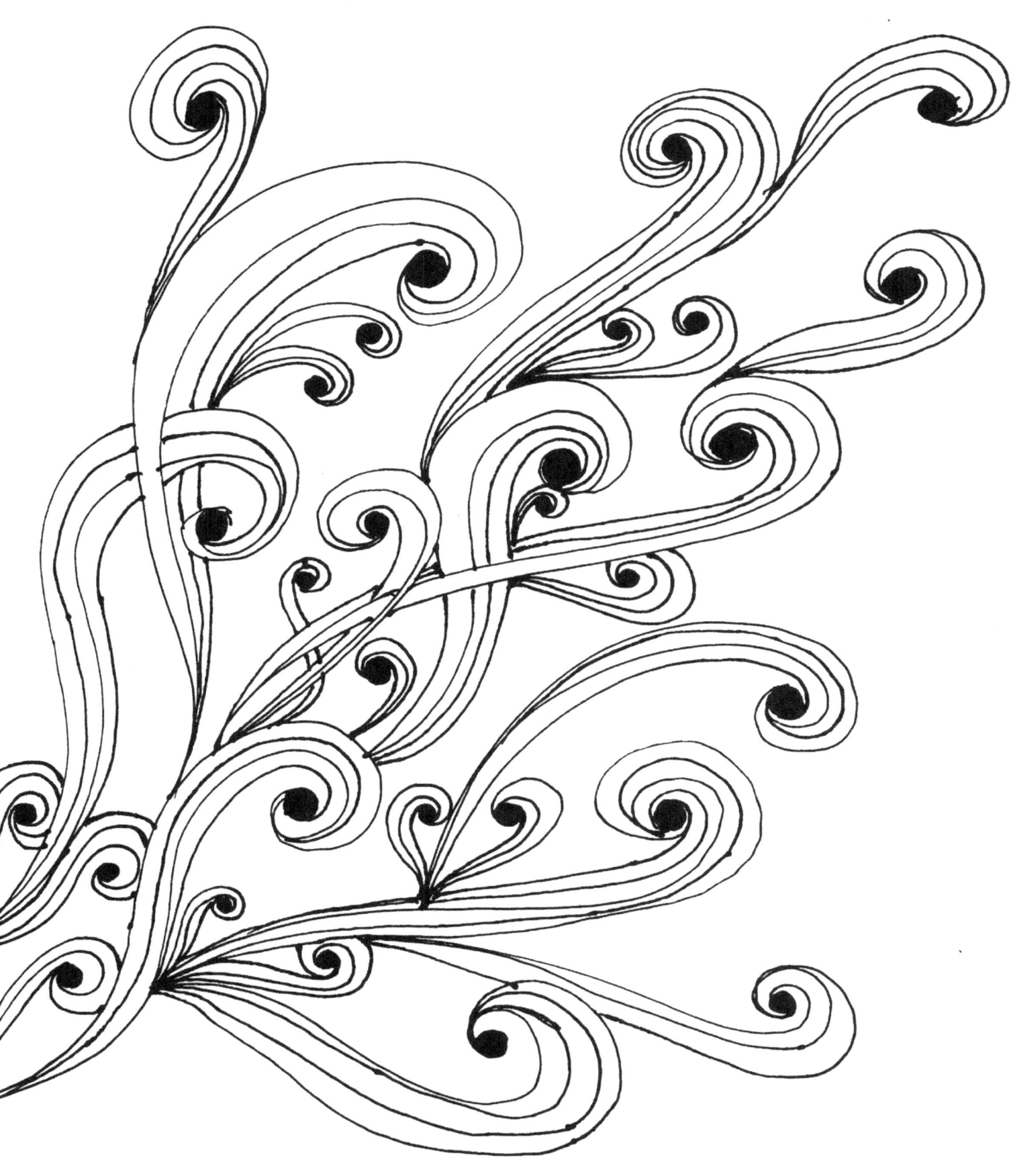

"Where the flowers bloom, so does hope."
~ Lady Bird Johnson

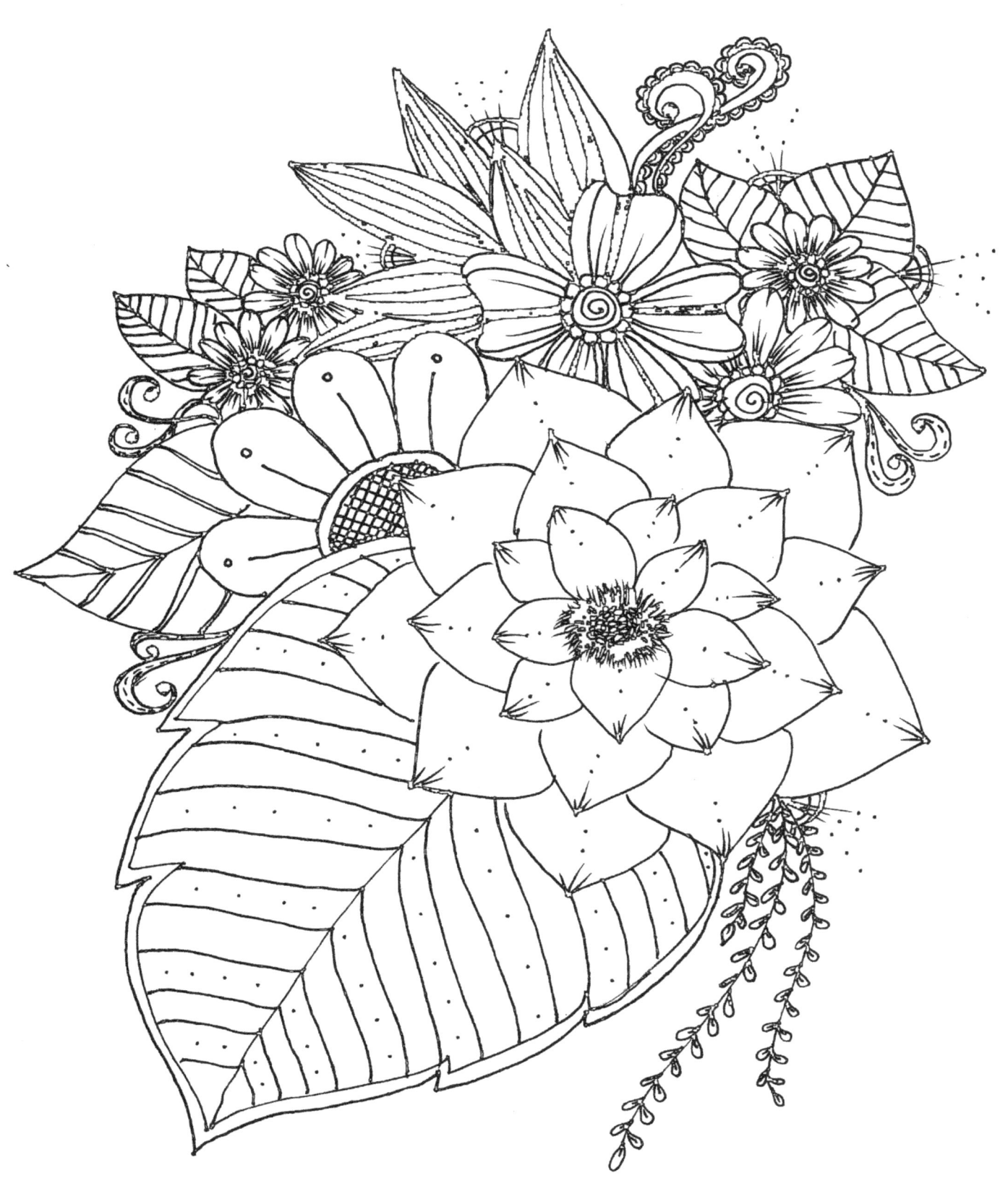

"Flowers are the music of the ground. From earth's lips spoken without sound."

~ Edwin Curran

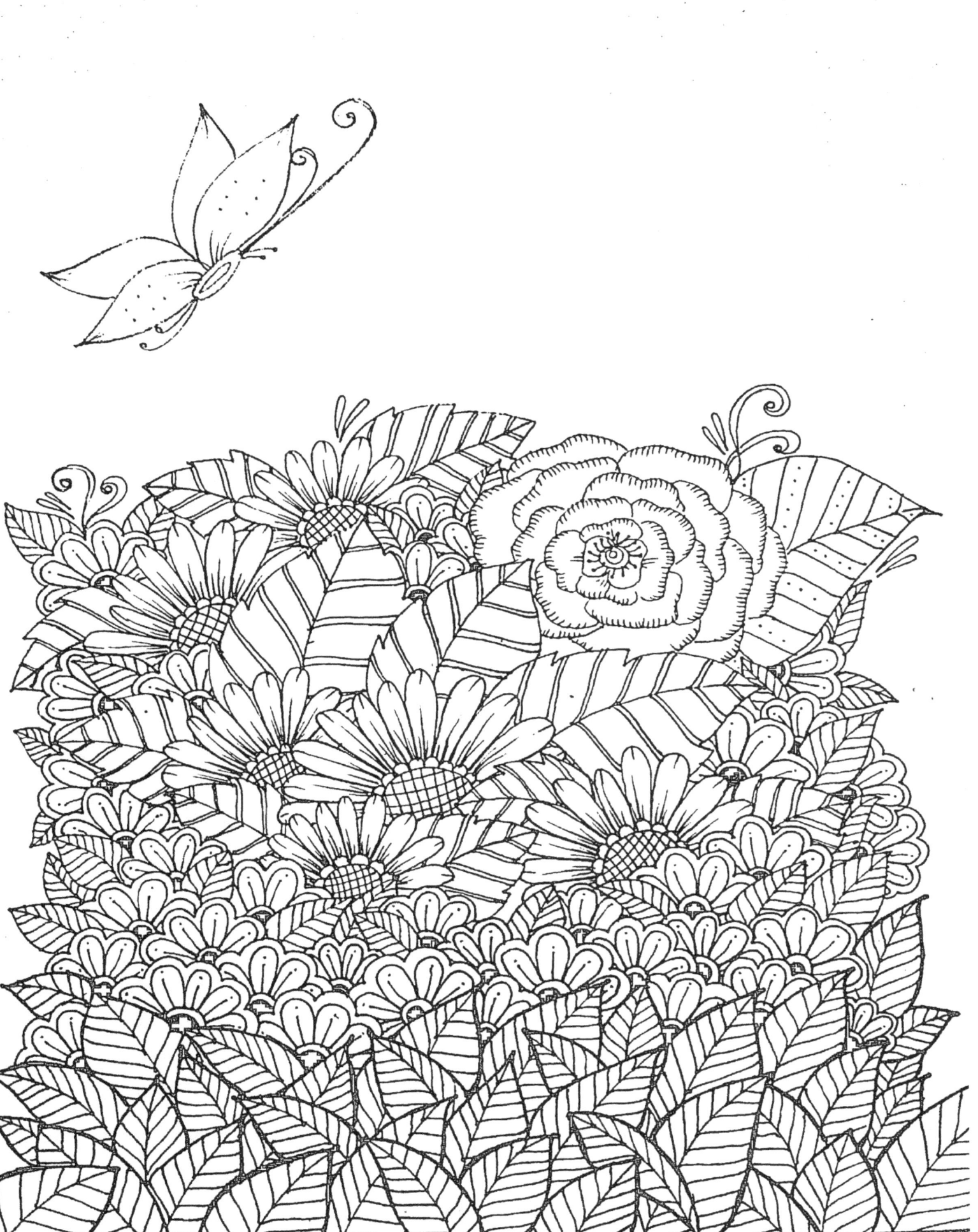

Thank you.

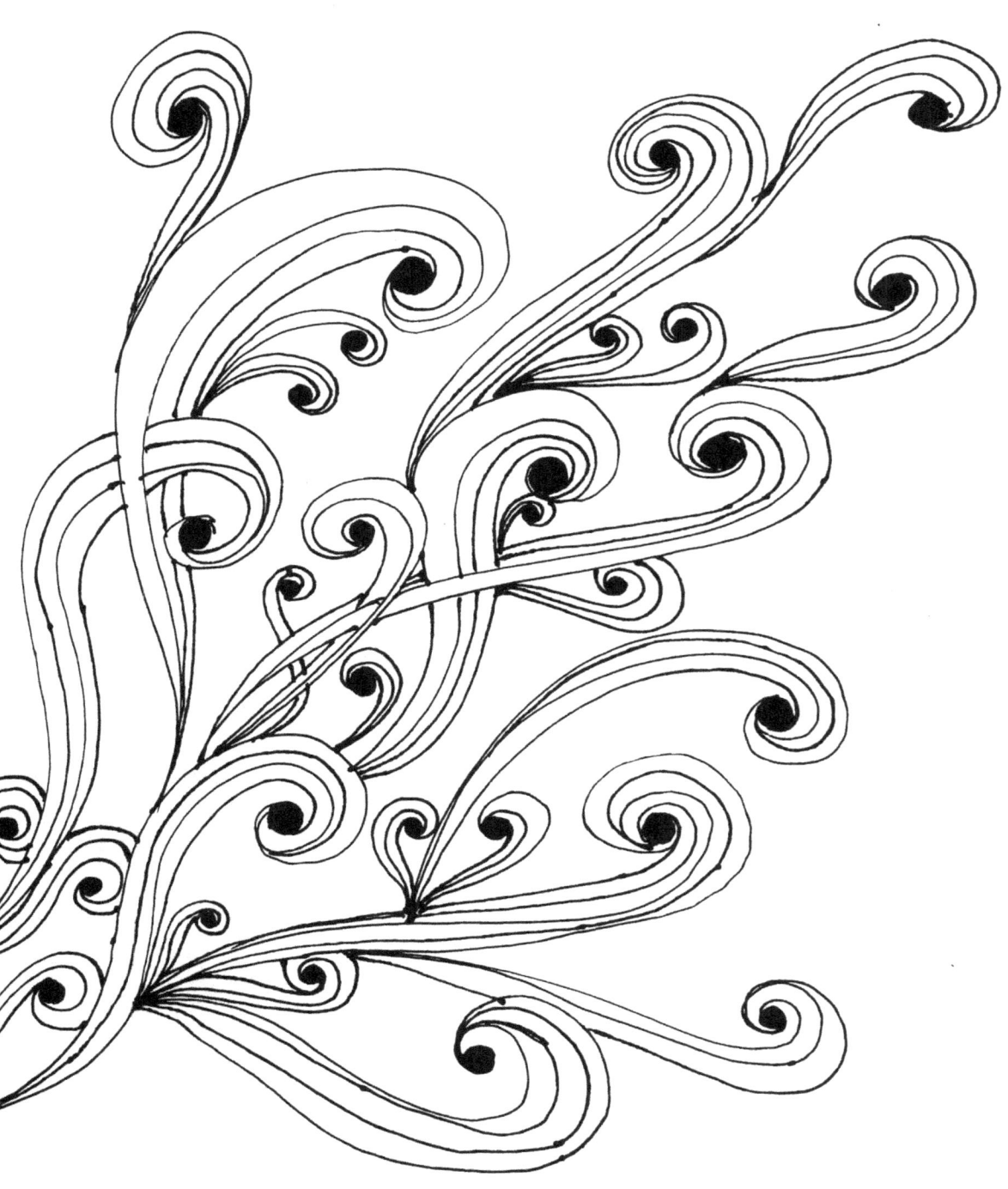